Vikings

Written By Don McLeese

Illustrated By Chris Marrinan

ROURKE PUBLISHING

Vero Beach, Florida 32964

www.rourkepublishing.com

Edited by Katherine M. Thal
Illustrated by Chris Marrinan
Art Direction and Page Layout by Renee Brady

Photo Credits: © espion: Title Page, 4, 5, 26, 27, 28, 29, 30, 31, 32; © Duncan Walker: 26; © Stephan Hoerold: 27; © Jan Rose: 29; © Stasyuk Stanislav: 28

Library of Congress Cataloging-in-Publication Data

McLeese, Don.
 Vikings / Don McLeese.
    p. cm. -- (Warriors graphic illustrated)
 Includes bibliographical references and index.
 ISBN 978-1-60694-434-9 (alk. paper)
 ISBN 978-1-60694-543-8 (soft cover)
 1. Vikings--Juvenile literature. 2. Norsemen--Juvenile literature. I. Title.
 DL66.M38 2010
 948'.02--dc22

                                     2009020495

Printed in the USA

CG/CG

www.rourkepublishing.com - rourke@rourkepublishing.com
Post Office Box 643328 Vero Beach, Florida 32964

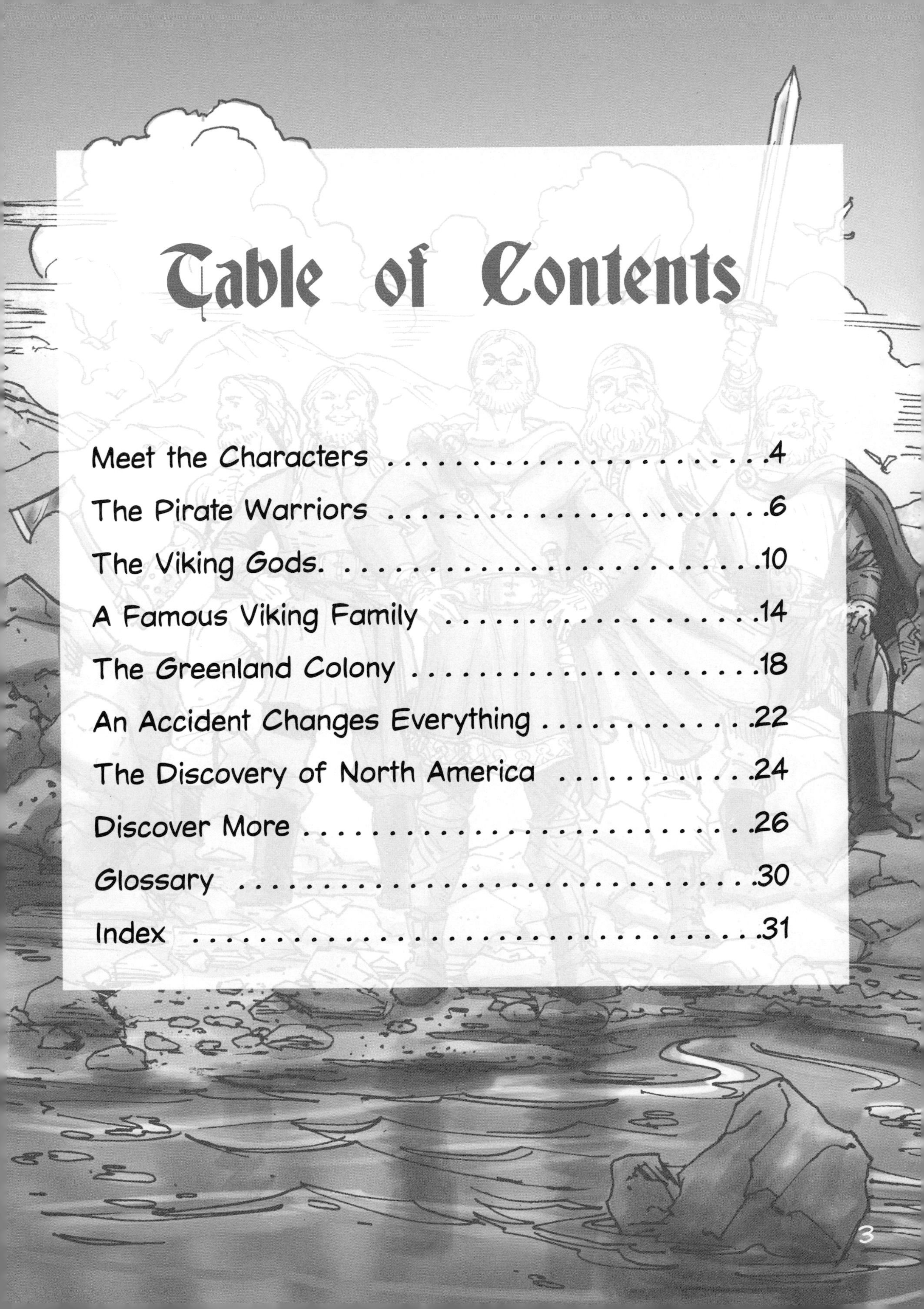

Table of Contents

Odin, Viking god

Odin has one eye, which blazes like the Sun. He is the god of war and death and also wisdom and poetry. He has the spear Gungnir, which never misses its target; the ring Draupnir, from which eight new rings appear every ninth night; and his eight-footed steed.

Thor, Viking god

Thor is portrayed as a large, powerful man with a red beard, and eyes of lightening.

Frey, Viking god

Frey rides a chariot pulled by a golden boar. He is the god of sun and rain, and the patron of bountiful harvests. He owns the ship Skidbladnir, or wooden-bladed. His ship always sails directly towards its target, and can become so small that it can fit in his pocket.

Freya, Viking goddess

Freya wears a beautiful cloak and a precious necklace. She rides a chariot pulled by two cats, and owns a battle boar named Hildesvini, which is actually her human lover Ottar in disguise.

Eric the Red

He was a Viking explorer who established a colony in Greenland. His real name was Eric Thorvaldson. His nickname came from his red hair, but he also had a very fiery temper.

Eric's parents

These were Eric the Red's parents. They lived in the south of what is now Norway. When Eric was ten years old, his father killed a man. The whole family had to flee to Iceland.

Thorgest

His name probably comes from the Viking god Thor. He fought with Eric the Red over a shovel, and Eric killed him.

Leif Ericson

Leif was Eric the Red's son. That is why his name was Ericson. He was a great explorer who likely landed on North America long before Christopher Columbus did.

Note: The characters in this book are based on real people and the mythical gods they believed in.

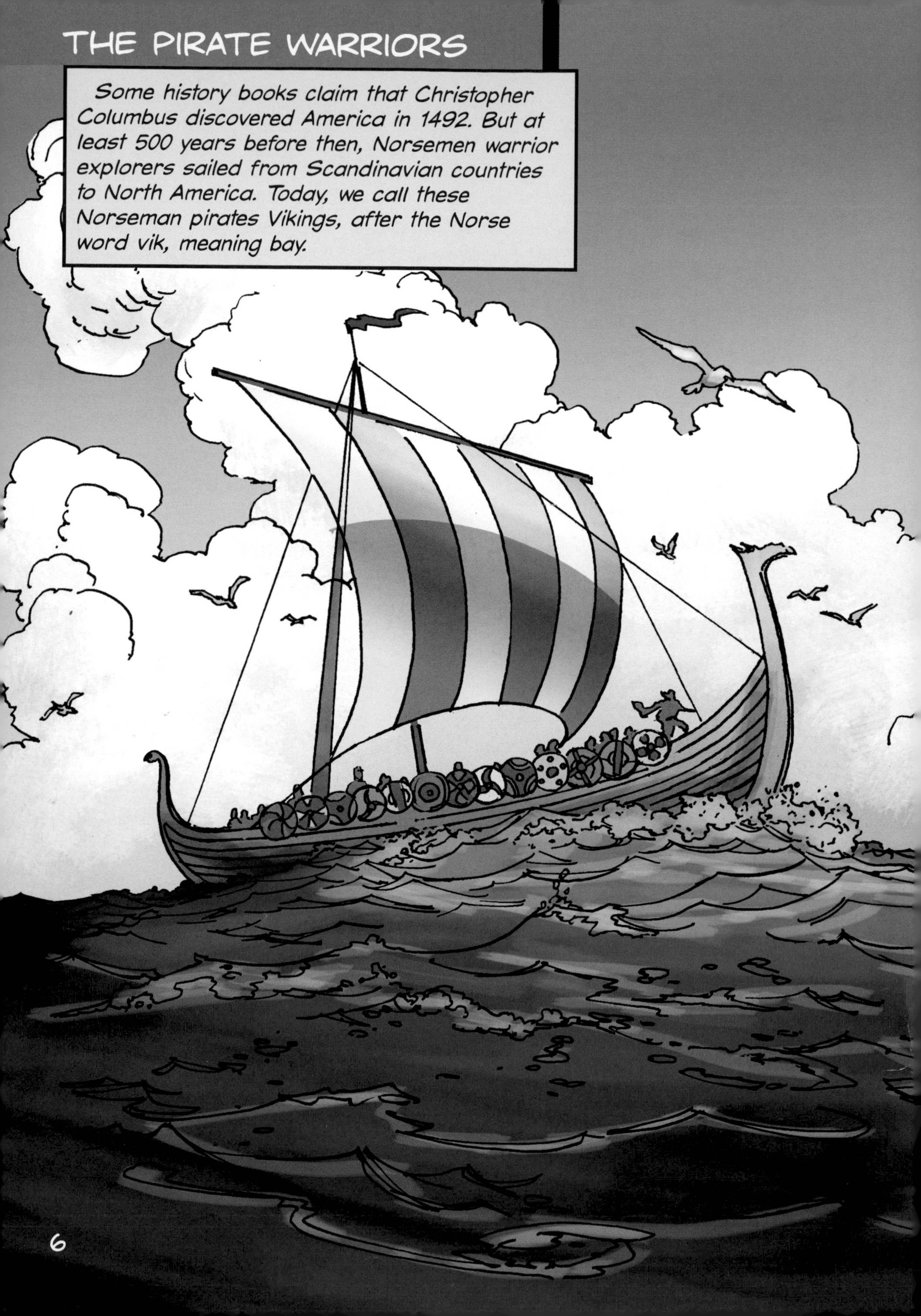
THE PIRATE WARRIORS
Some history books claim that Christopher Columbus discovered America in 1492. But at least 500 years before then, Norsemen warrior explorers sailed from Scandinavian countries to North America. Today, we call these Norseman pirates Vikings, after the Norse word vik, meaning bay.

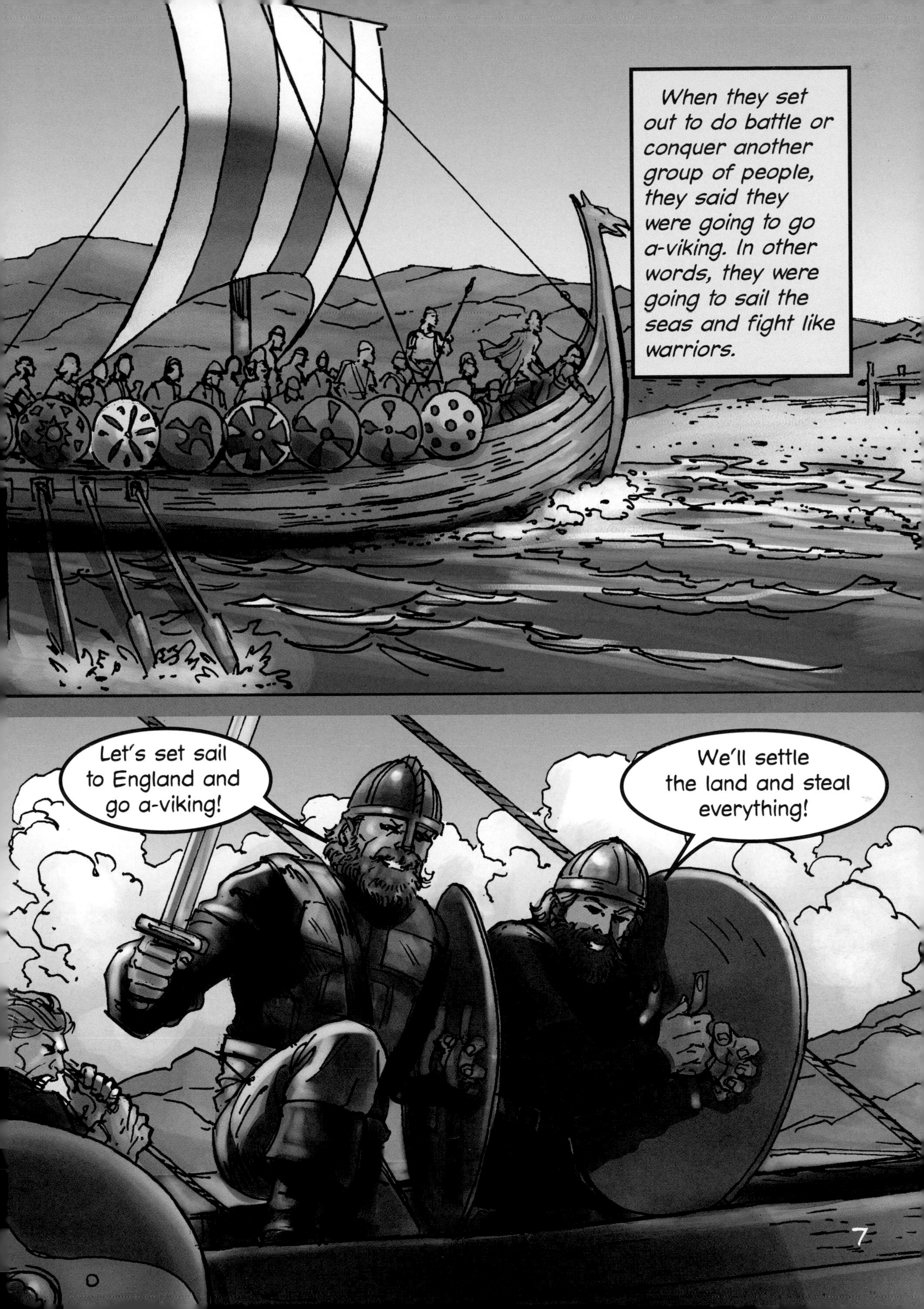
When they set out to do battle or conquer another group of people, they said they were going to go a-viking. In other words, they were going to sail the seas and fight like warriors.
Let's set sail to England and go a-viking!
We'll settle the land and steal everything!

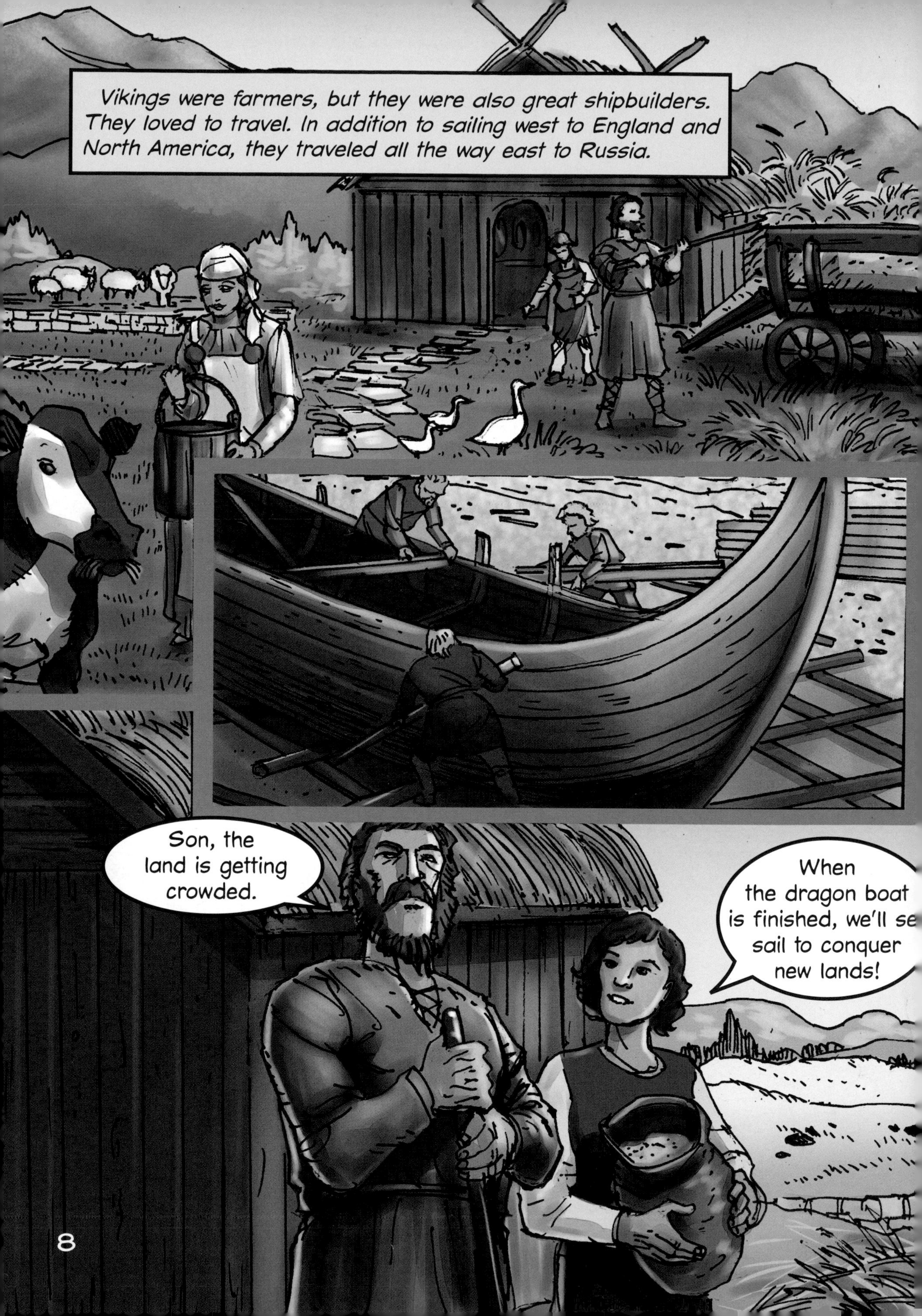
Vikings were farmers, but they were also great shipbuilders. They loved to travel. In addition to sailing west to England and North America, they traveled all the way east to Russia.
Son, the land is getting crowded.
When the dragon boat is finished, we'll se sail to conquer new lands!

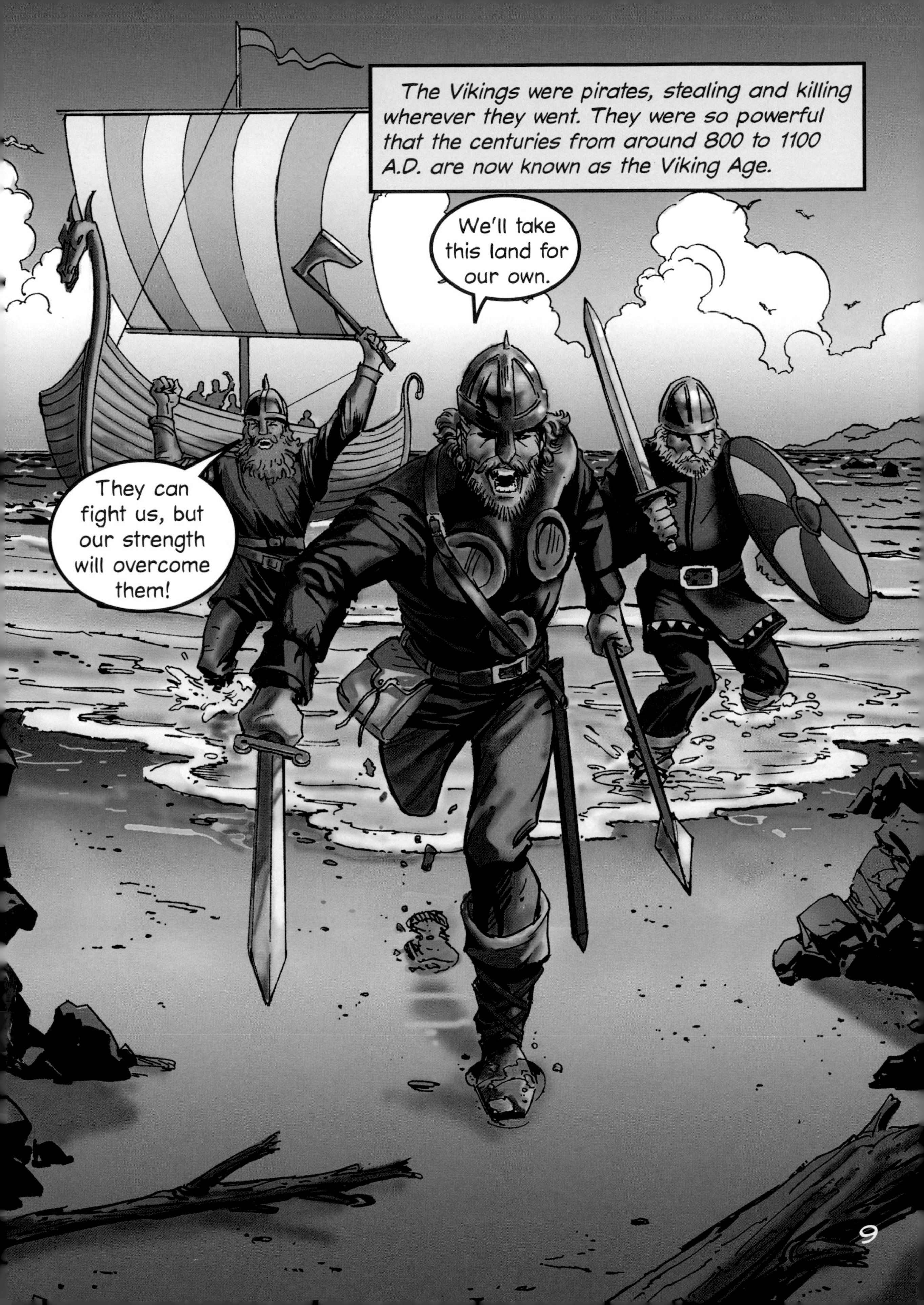
The Vikings were pirates, stealing and killing wherever they went. They were so powerful that the centuries from around 800 to 1100 A.D. are now known as the Viking Age.
We'll take this land for our own.
They can fight us, but our strength will overcome them!

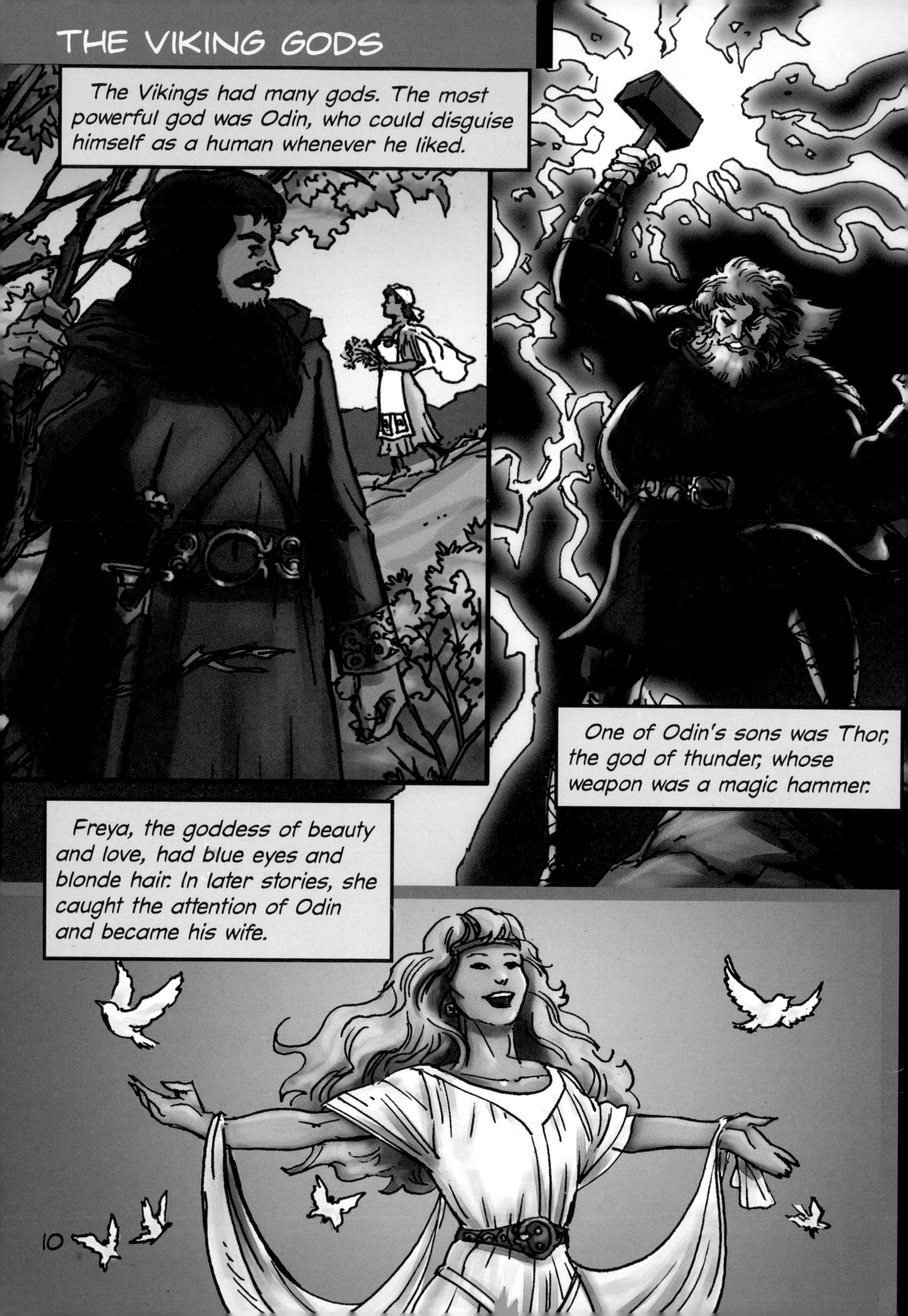
THE VIKING GODS
The Vikings had many gods. The most powerful god was Odin, who could disguise himself as a human whenever he liked.
One of Odin's sons was Thor, the god of thunder, whose weapon was a magic hammer.
Freya, the goddess of beauty and love, had blue eyes and blonde hair. In later stories, she caught the attention of Odin and became his wife.

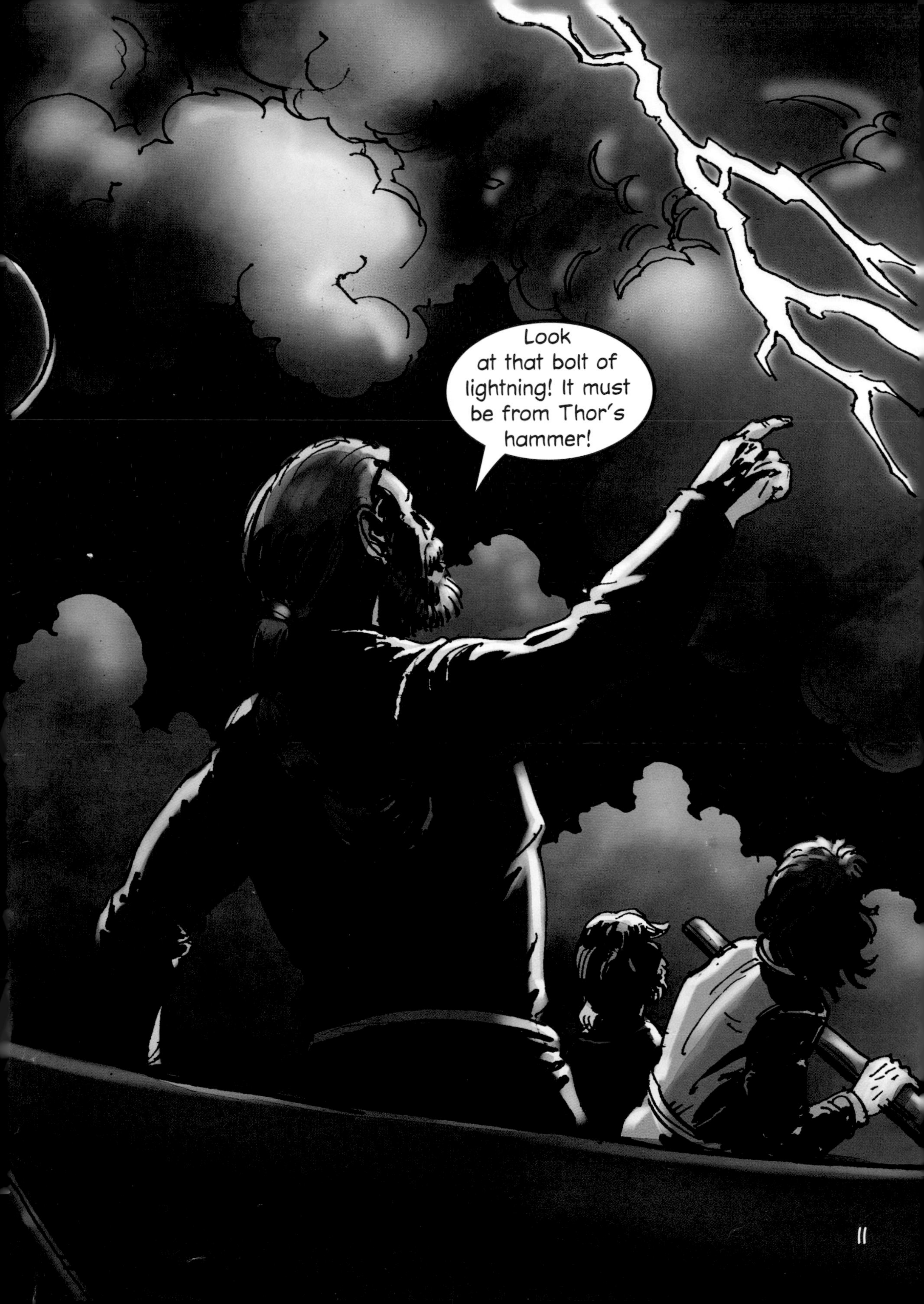
Look at that bolt of lightning! It must be from Thor's hammer!

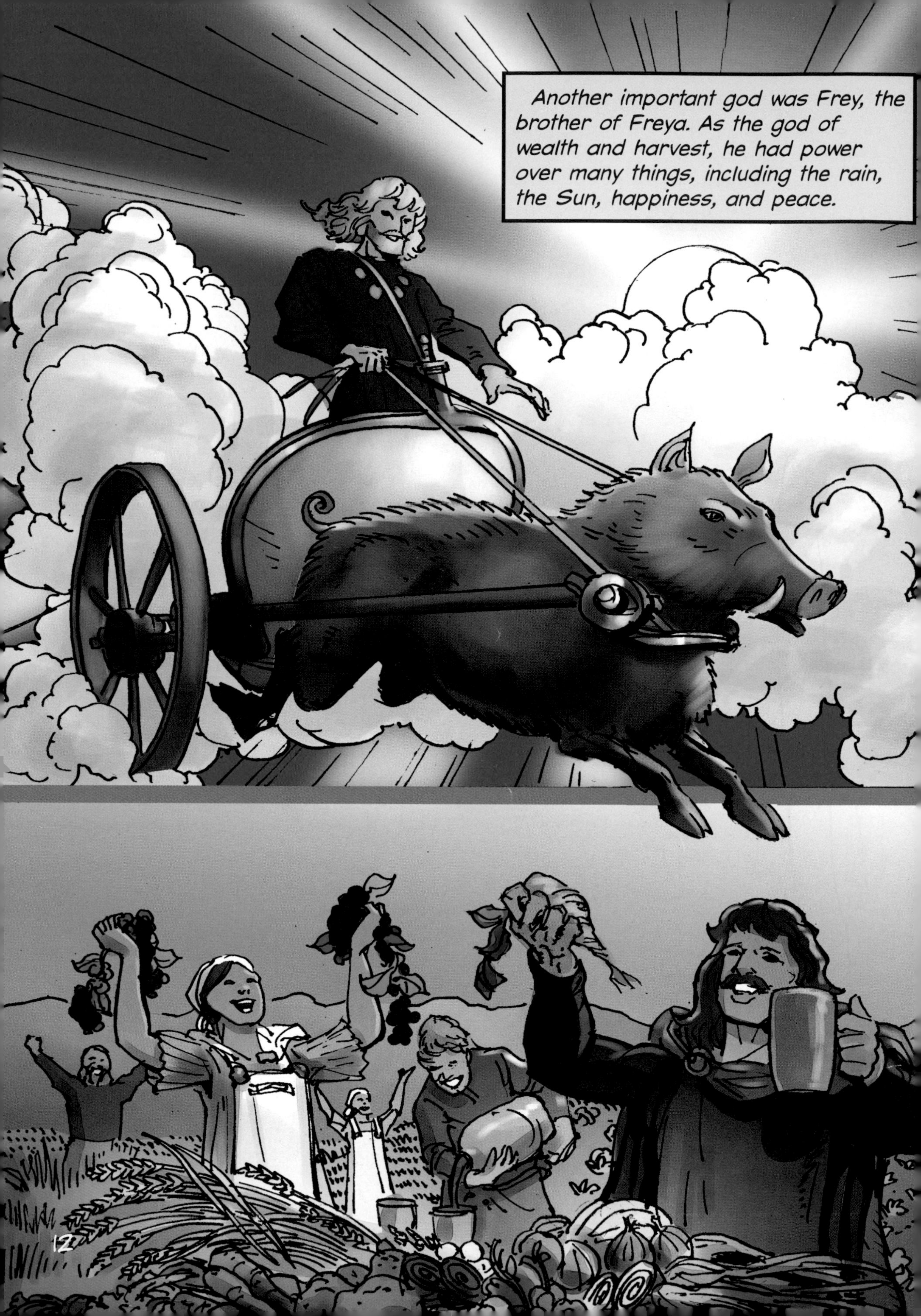
Another important god was Frey, the brother of Freya. As the god of wealth and harvest, he had power over many things, including the rain, the Sun, happiness, and peace.

Though no one believes in these gods anymore, we remember them through our days of the week. After the Vikings invaded England, Wednesday was named for Odin's day, Thursday was from Thor's day, and Friday honored Frey and Freya.

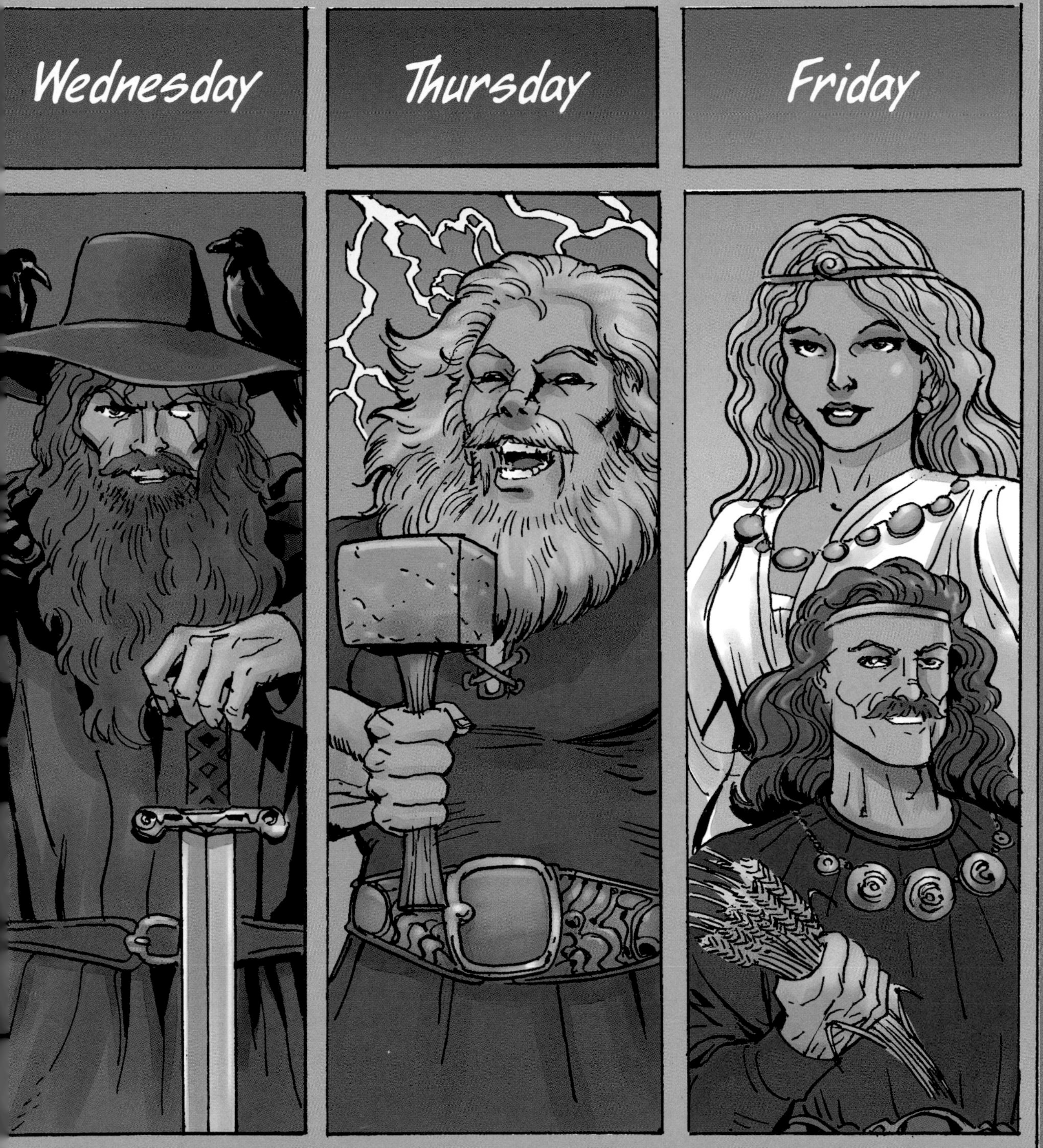

Wednesday
Thursday
Friday

A FAMOUS VIKING FAMILY

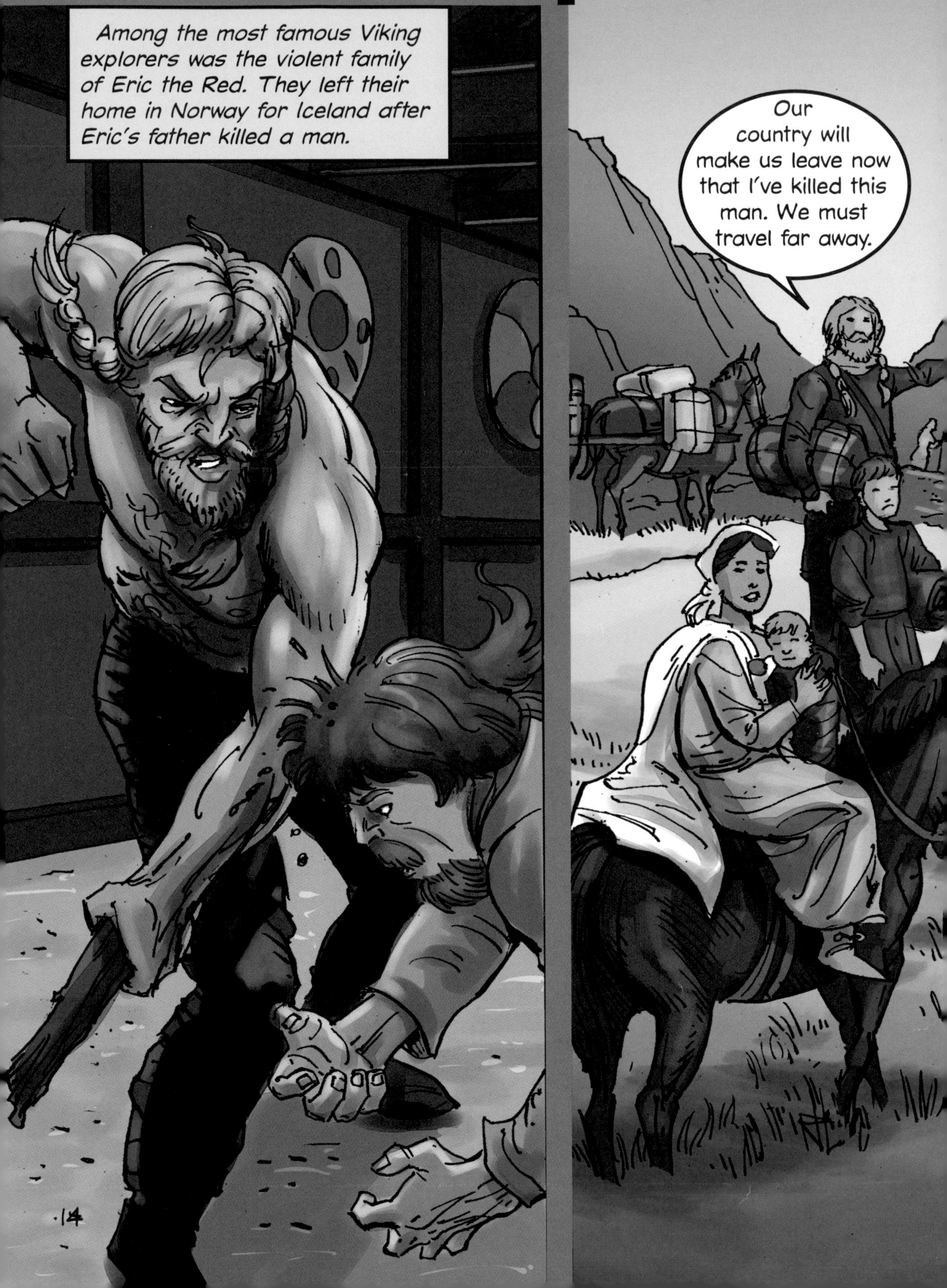
Among the most famous Viking explorers was the violent family of Eric the Red. They left their home in Norway for Iceland after Eric's father killed a man.
Our country will make us leave now that I've killed this man. We must travel far away.

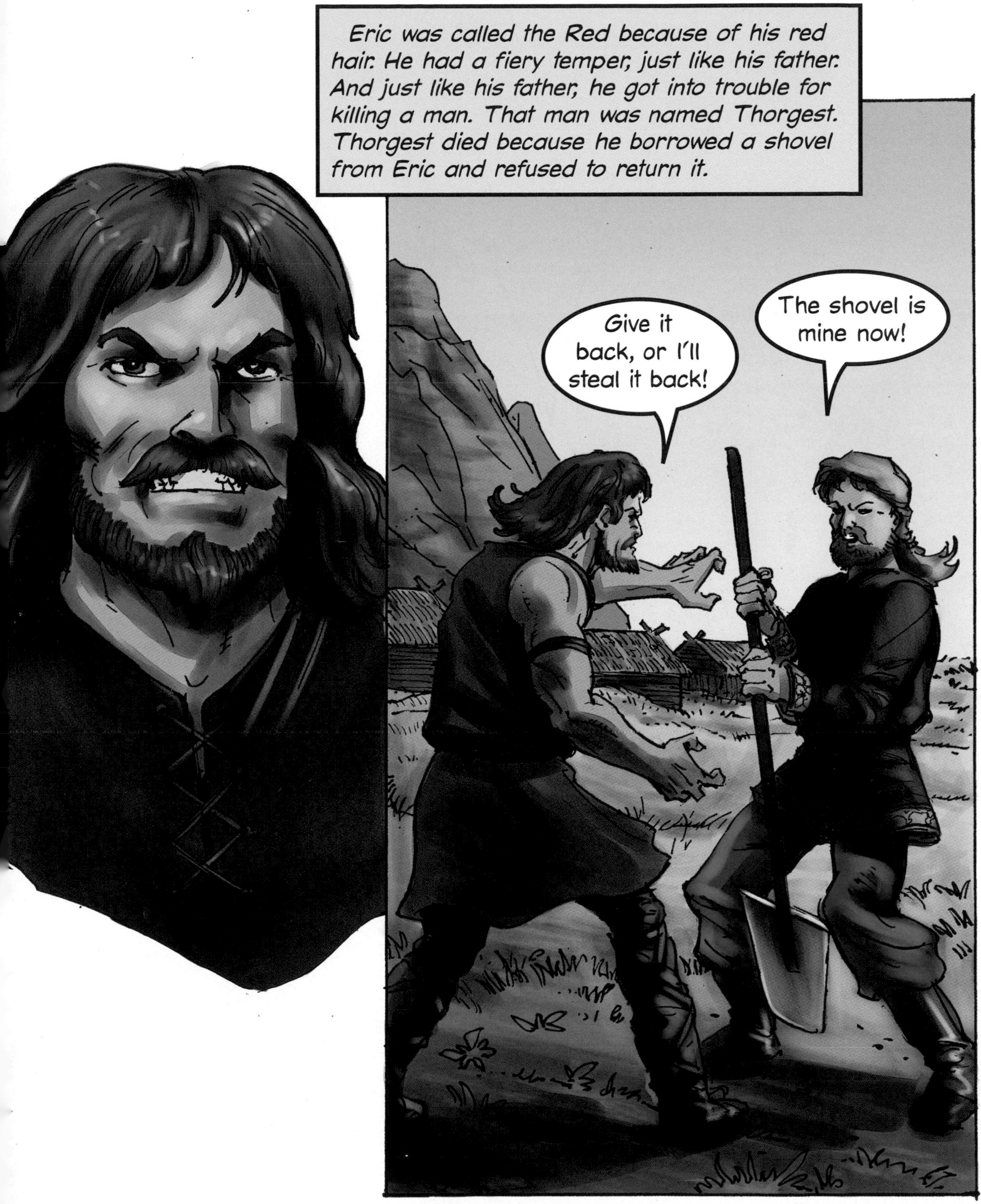
Eric was called the Red because of his red hair. He had a fiery temper, just like his father. And just like his father, he got into trouble for killing a man. That man was named Thorgest. Thorgest died because he borrowed a shovel from Eric and refused to return it.
Give it back, or I'll steal it back!
The shovel is mine now!

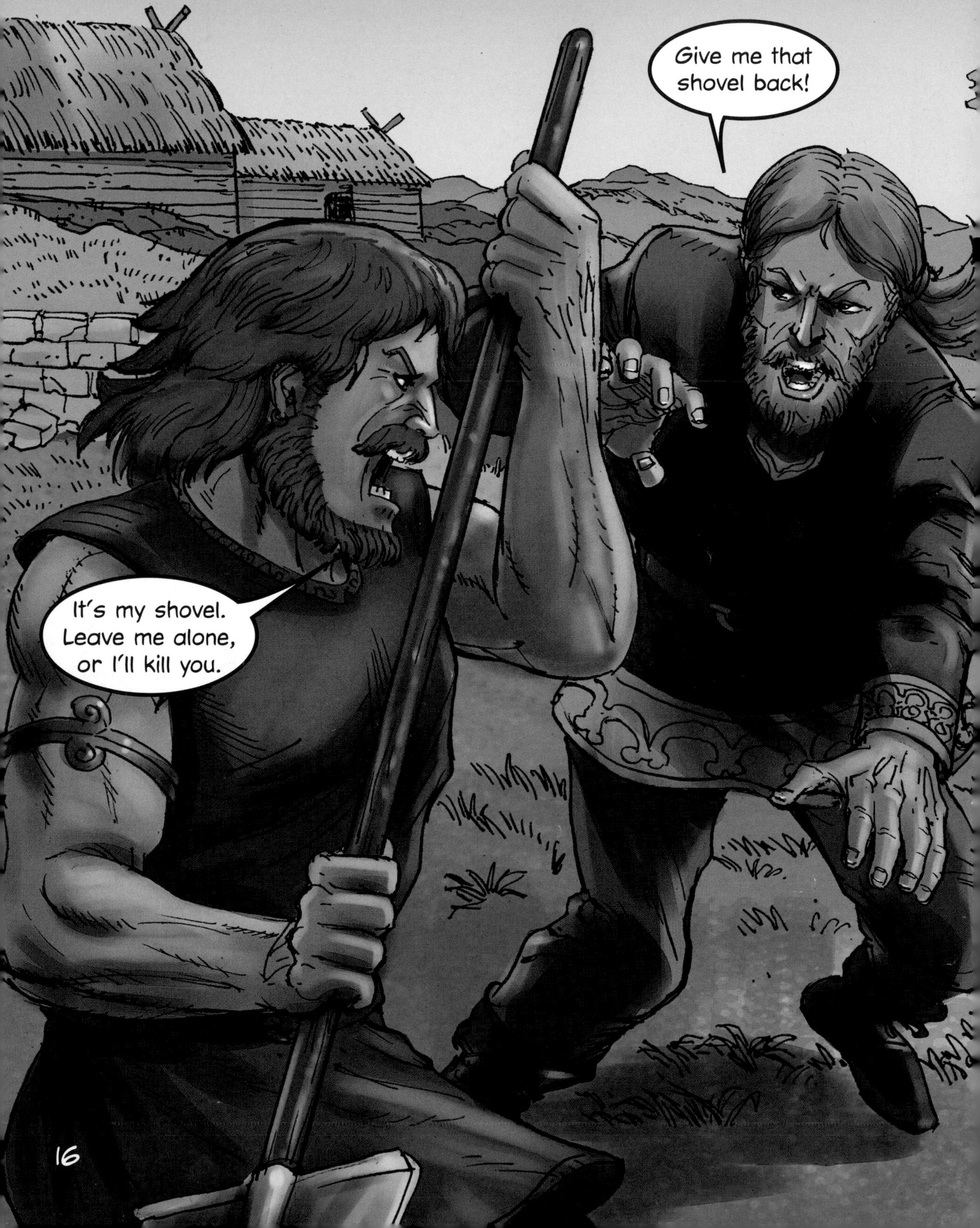
Give me that shovel back!
It's my shovel. Leave me alone, or I'll kill you.

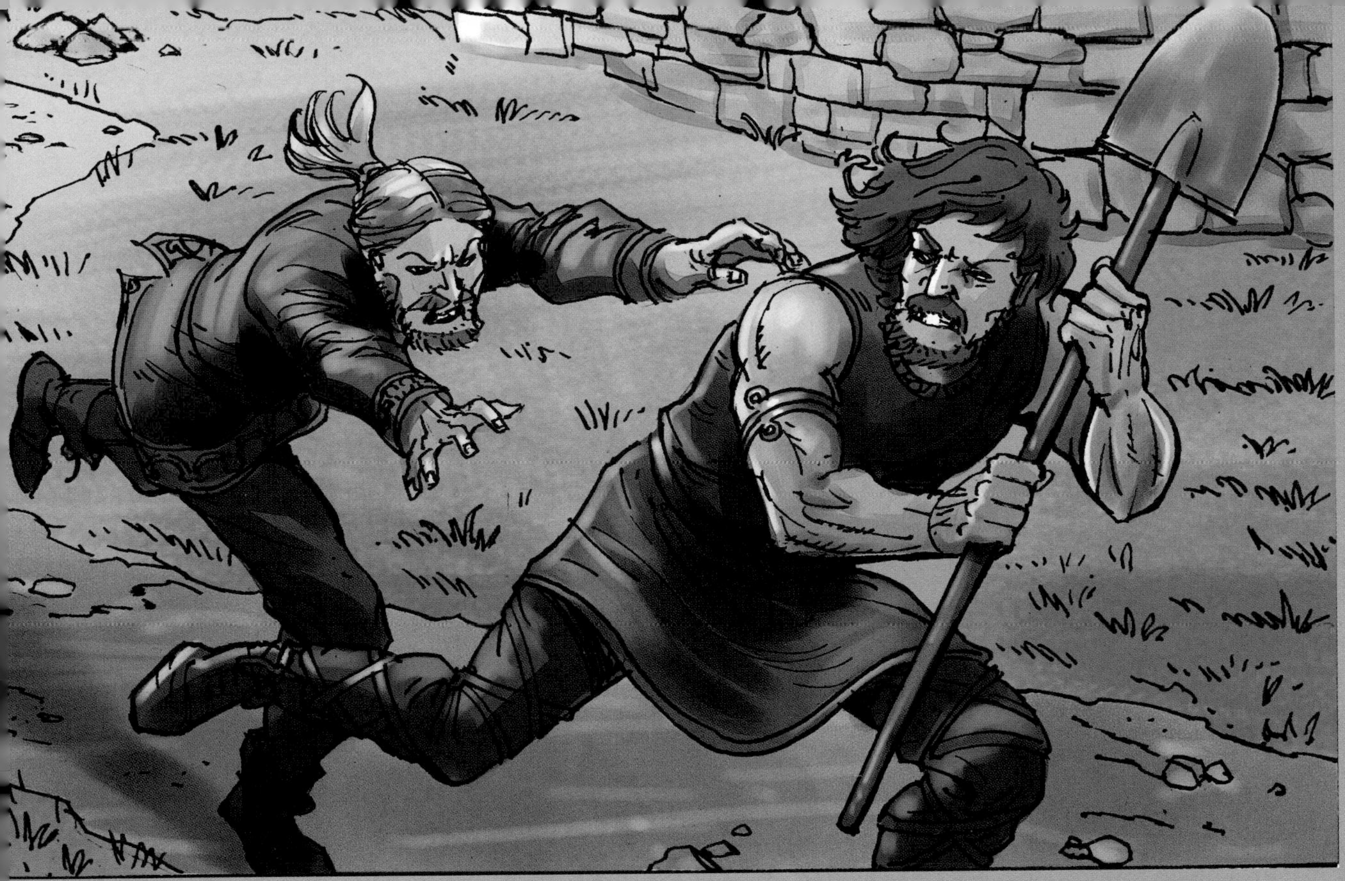

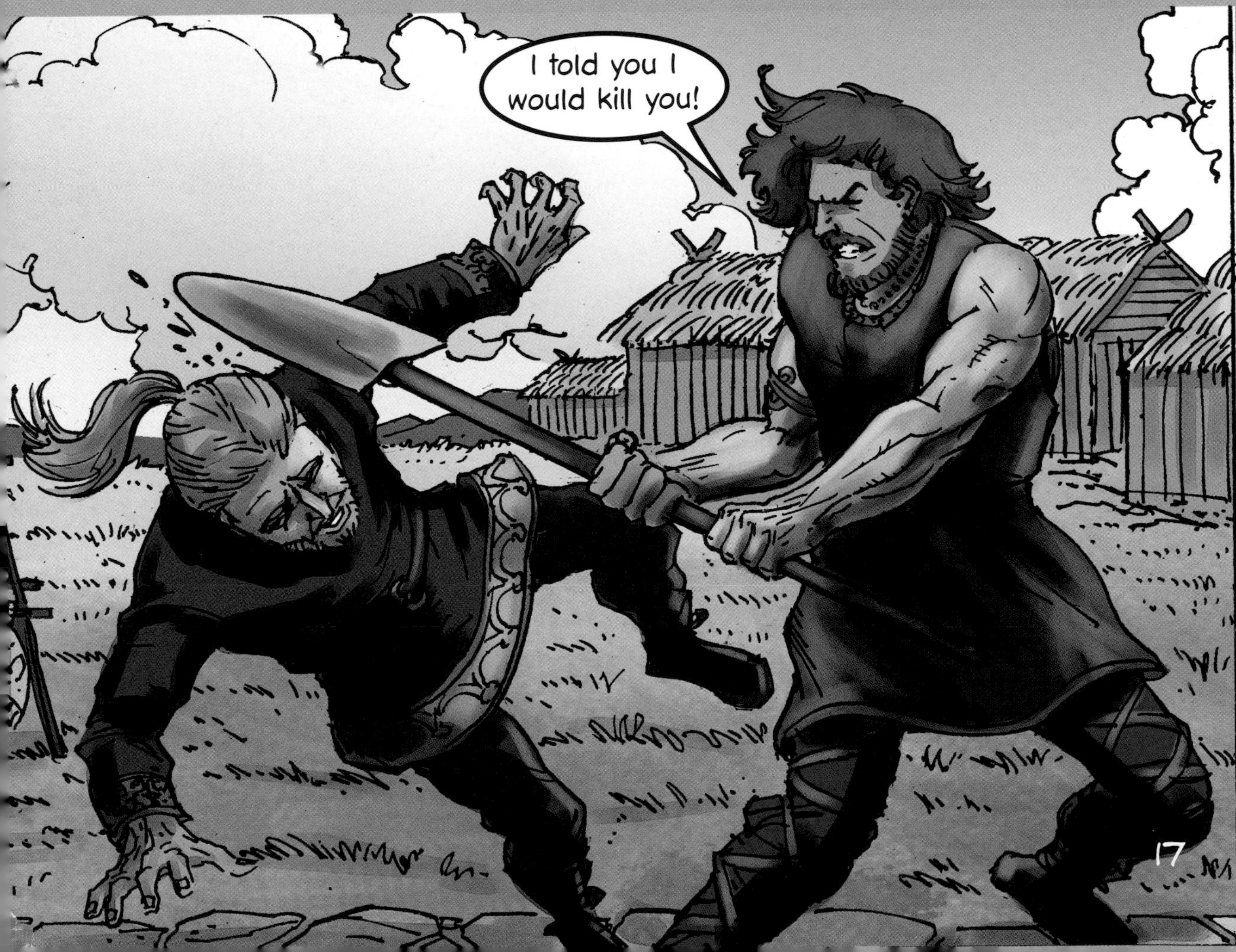
I told you I would kill you!

THE GREENLAND COLONY

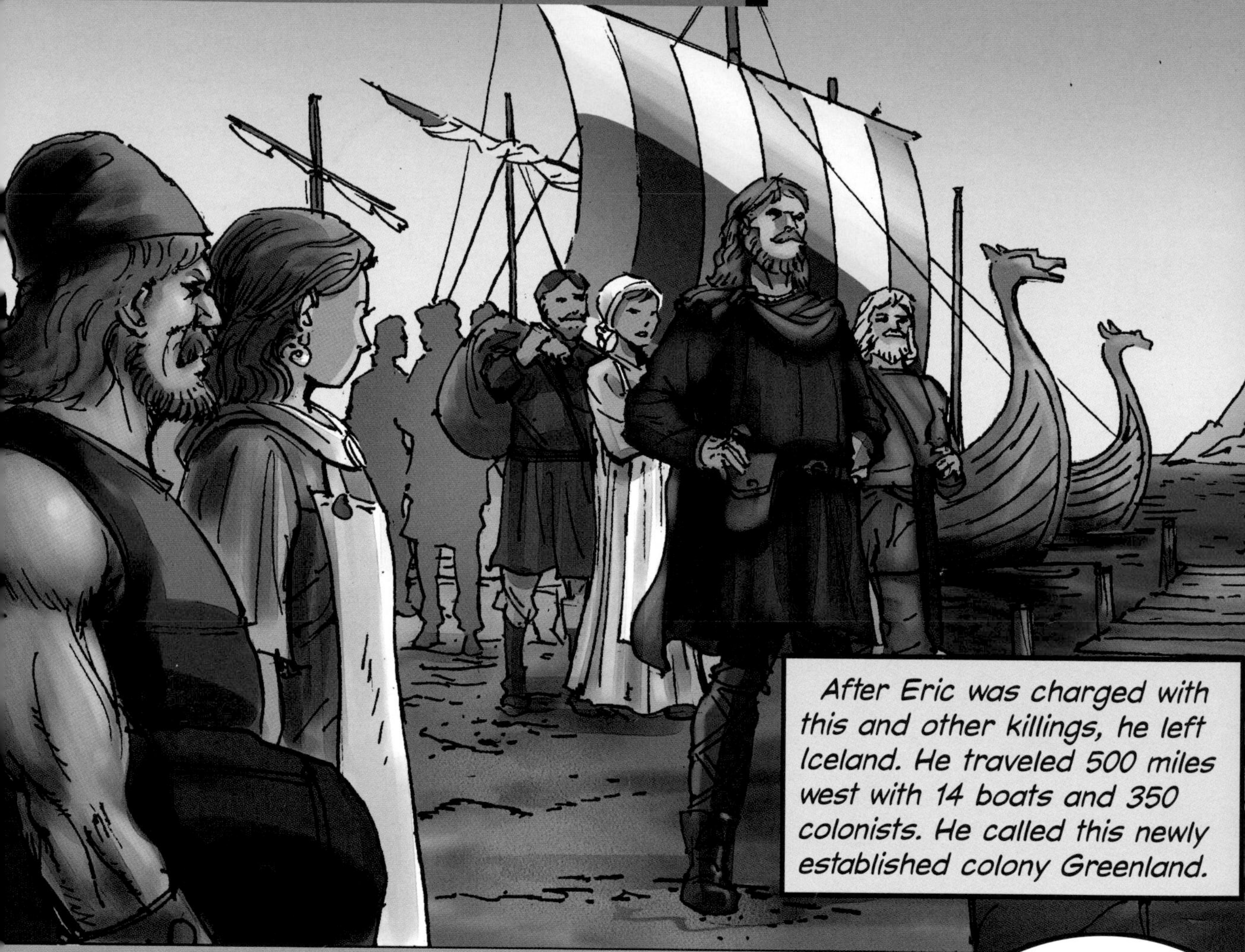
After Eric was charged with this and other killings, he left Iceland. He traveled 500 miles west with 14 boats and 350 colonists. He called this newly established colony Greenland.

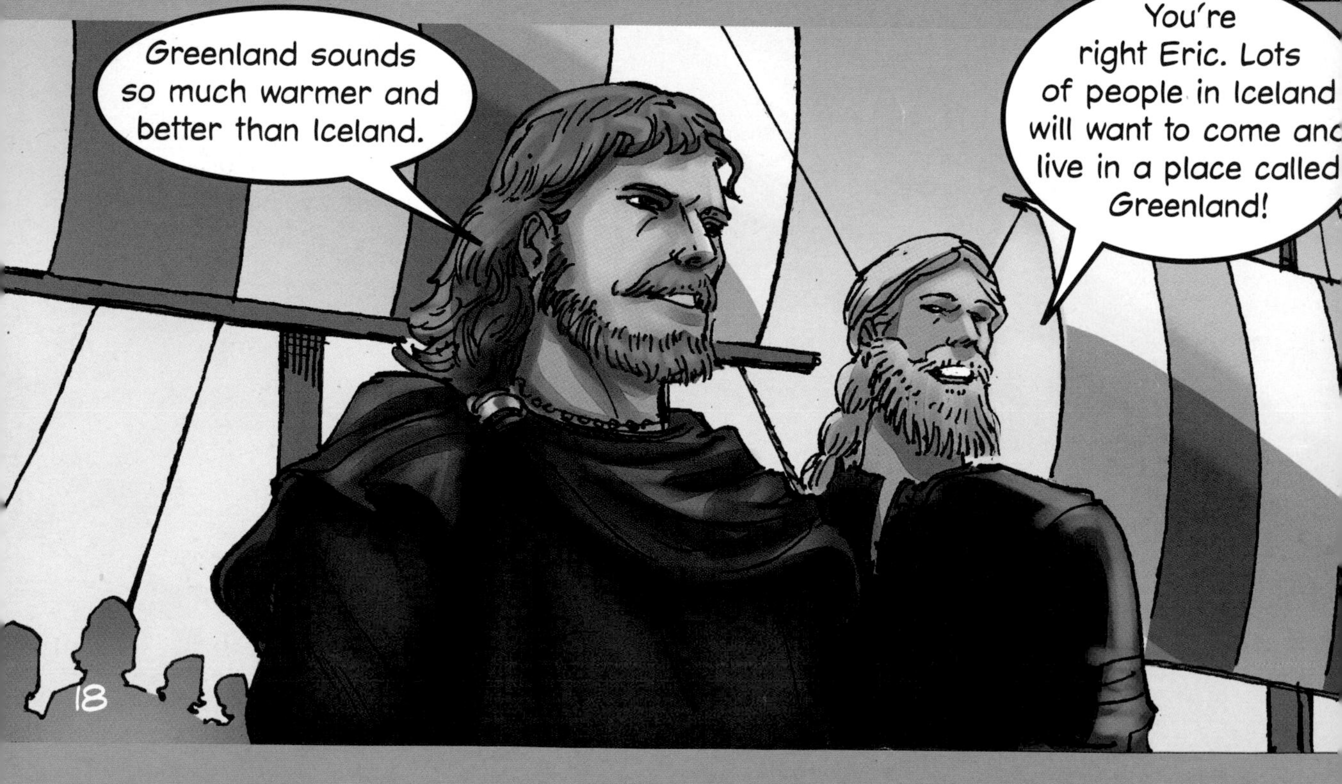
Greenland sounds so much warmer and better than Iceland.
You're right Eric. Lots of people in Iceland will want to come anc live in a place called Greenland!

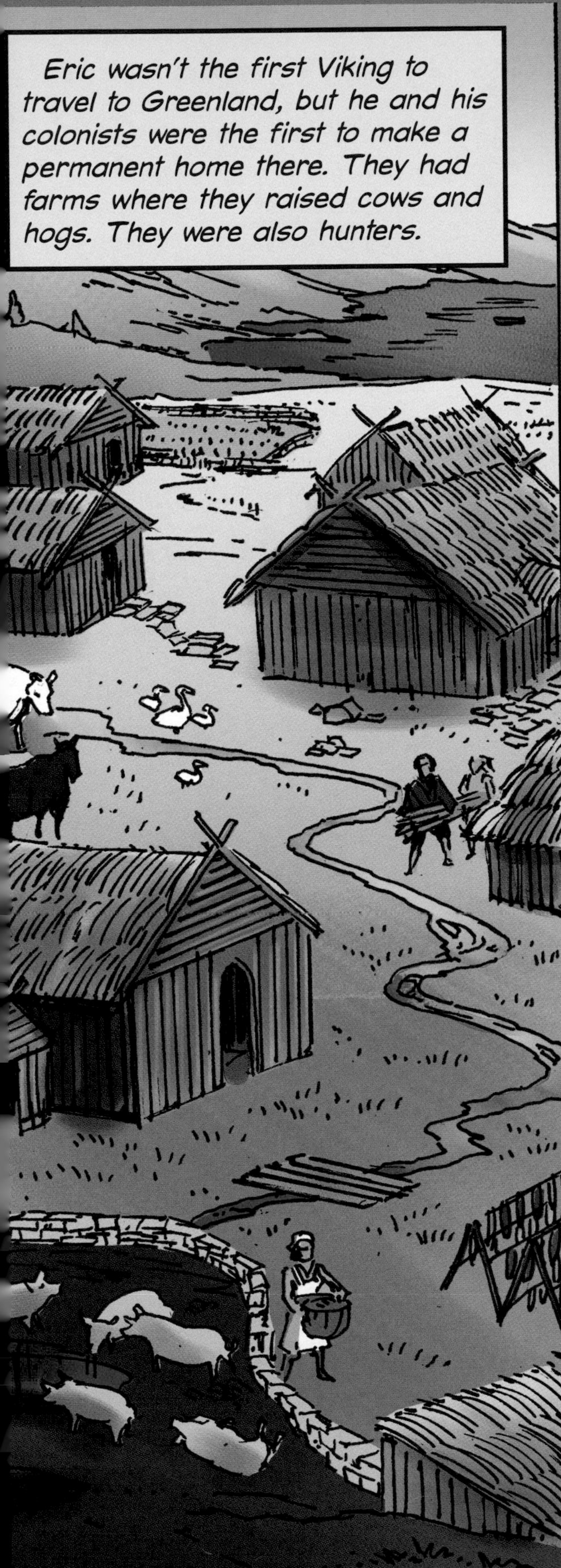
Eric wasn't the first Viking to travel to Greenland, but he and his colonists were the first to make a permanent home there. They had farms where they raised cows and hogs. They were also hunters.

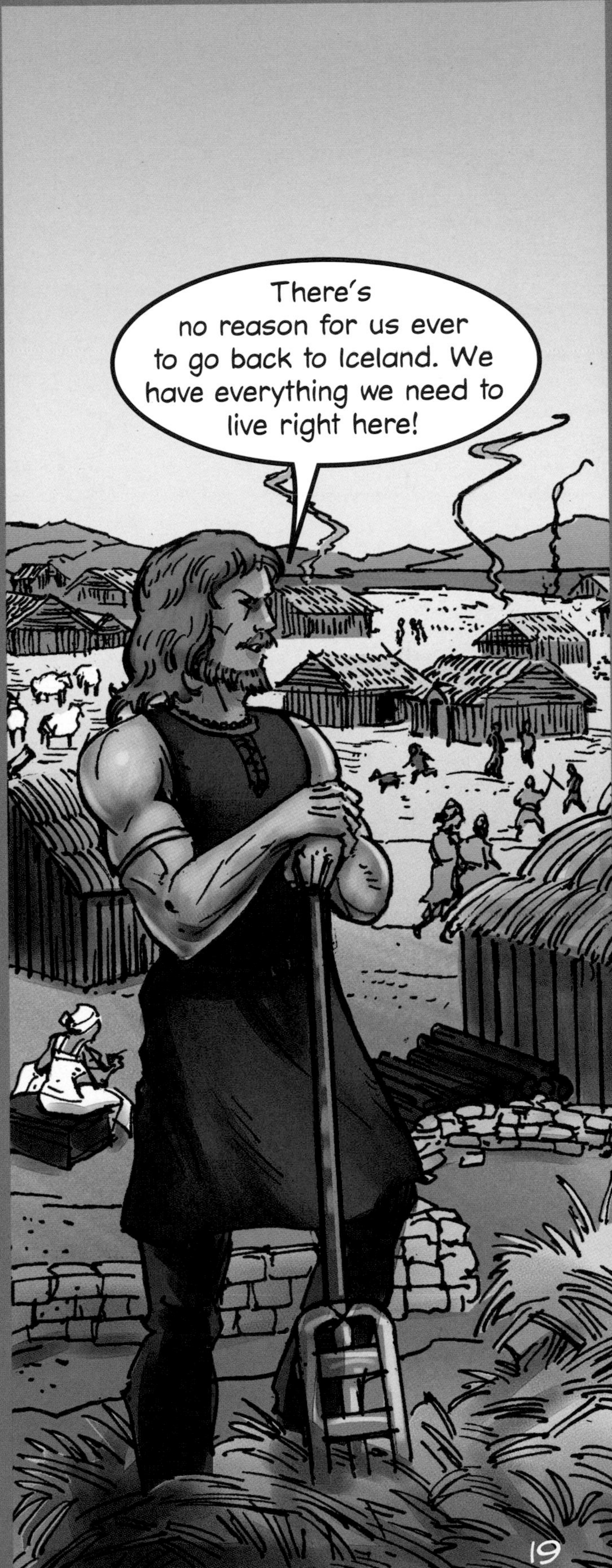
There's no reason for us ever to go back to Iceland. We have everything we need to live right here!

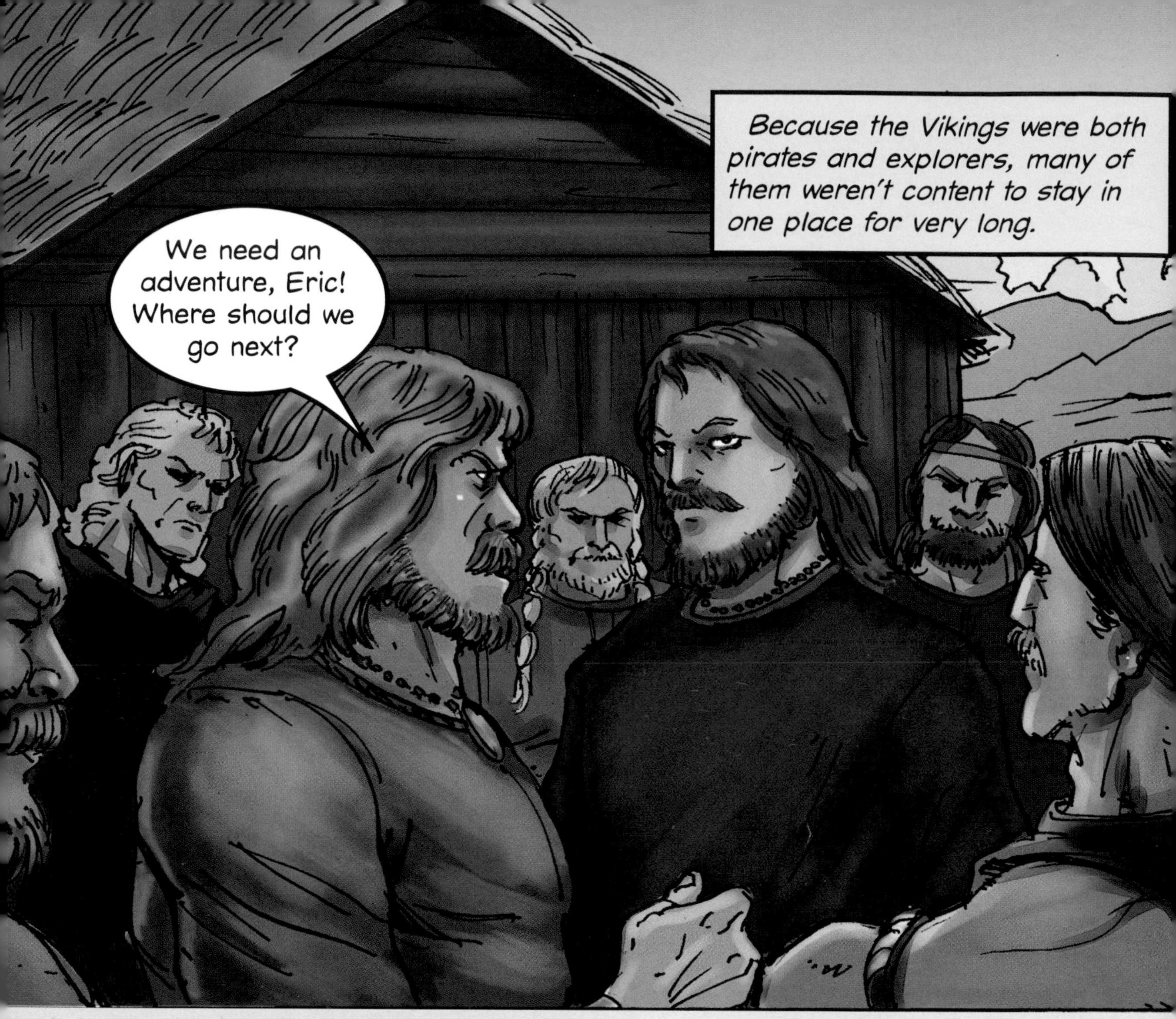
Because the Vikings were both pirates and explorers, many of them weren't content to stay in one place for very long.
We need an adventure, Eric! Where should we go next?

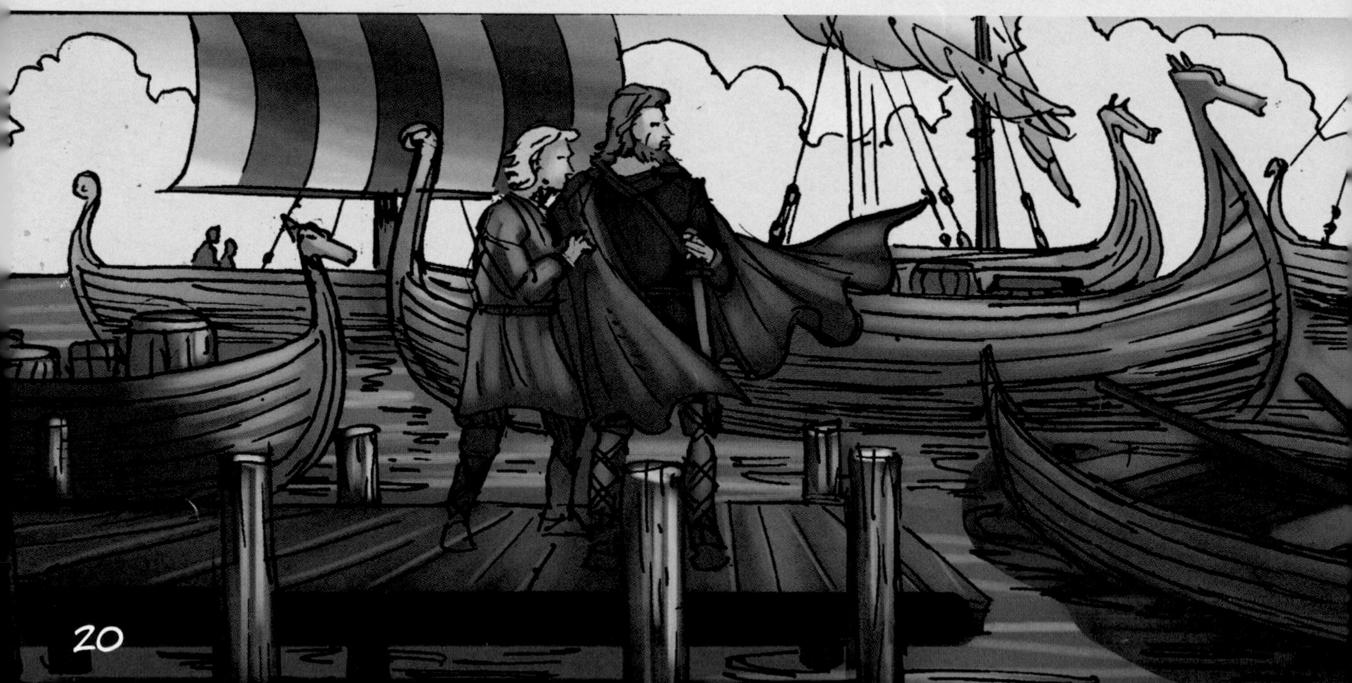

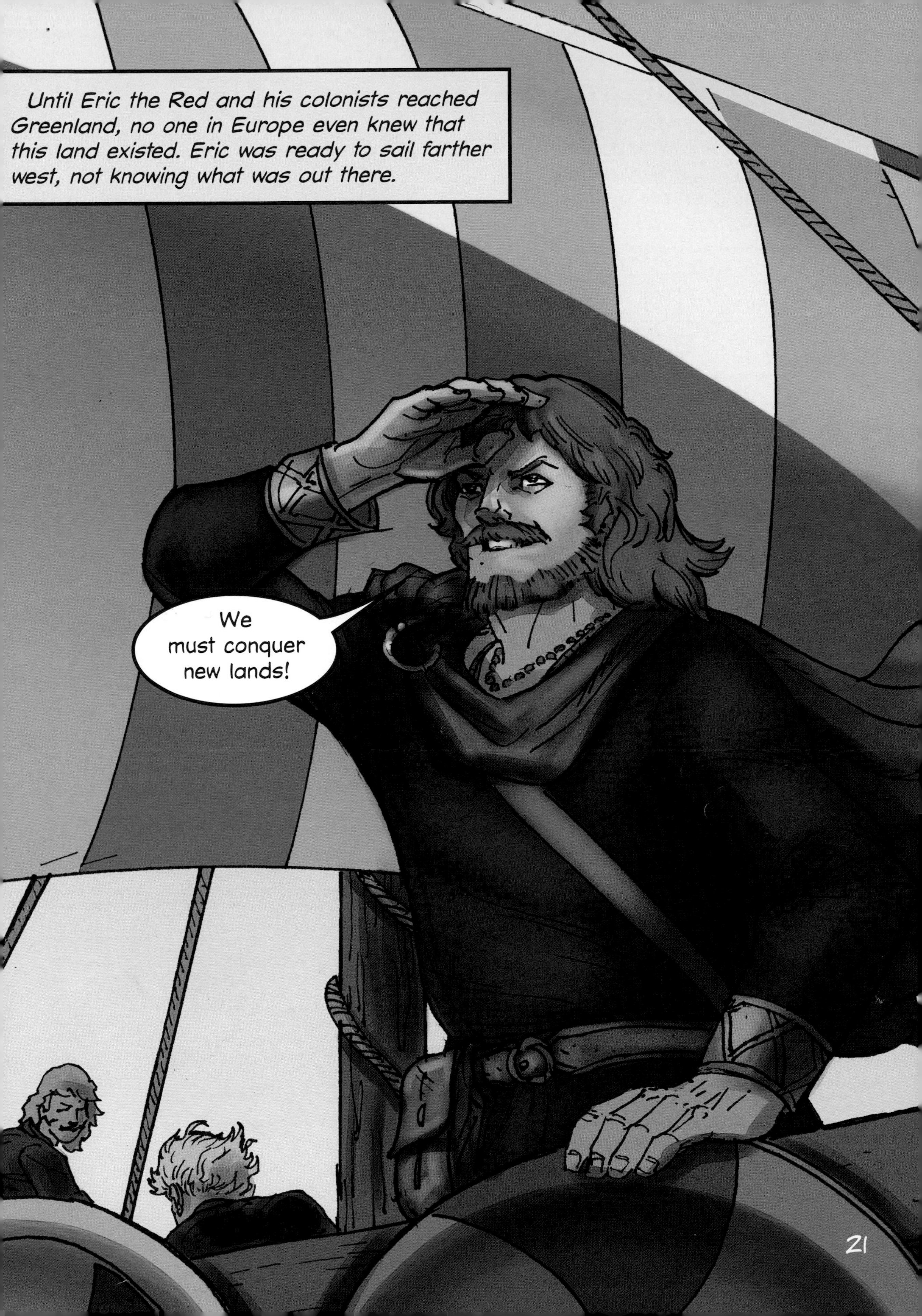
Until Eric the Red and his colonists reached Greenland, no one in Europe even knew that this land existed. Eric was ready to sail farther west, not knowing what was out there.
We must conquer new lands!

AN ACCIDENT CHANGES EVERYTHING

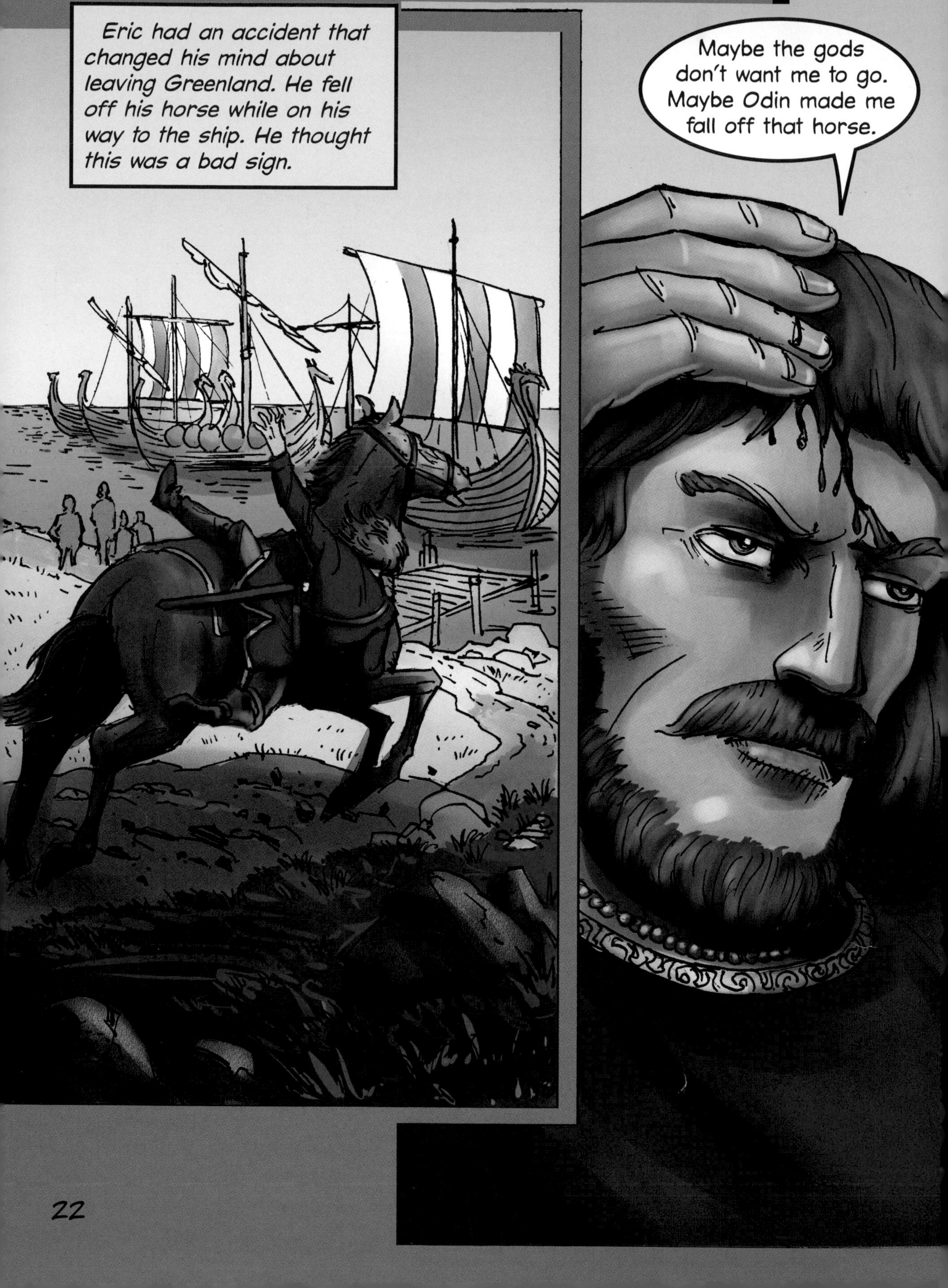
Eric had an accident that changed his mind about leaving Greenland. He fell off his horse while on his way to the ship. He thought this was a bad sign.
Maybe the gods don't want me to go. Maybe Odin made me fall off that horse.

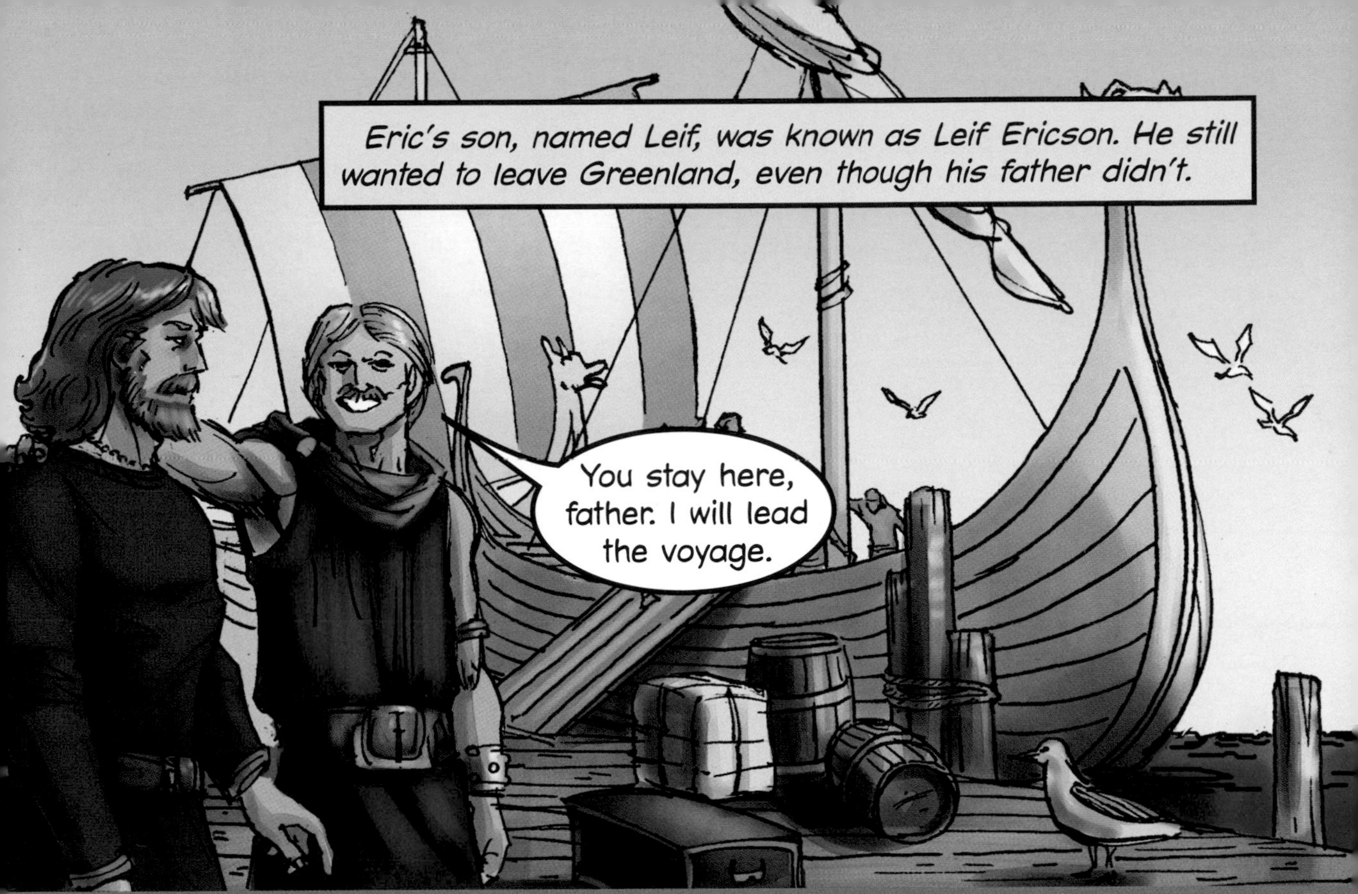
Eric's son, named Leif, was known as Leif Ericson. He still wanted to leave Greenland, even though his father didn't.
You stay here, father. I will lead the voyage.

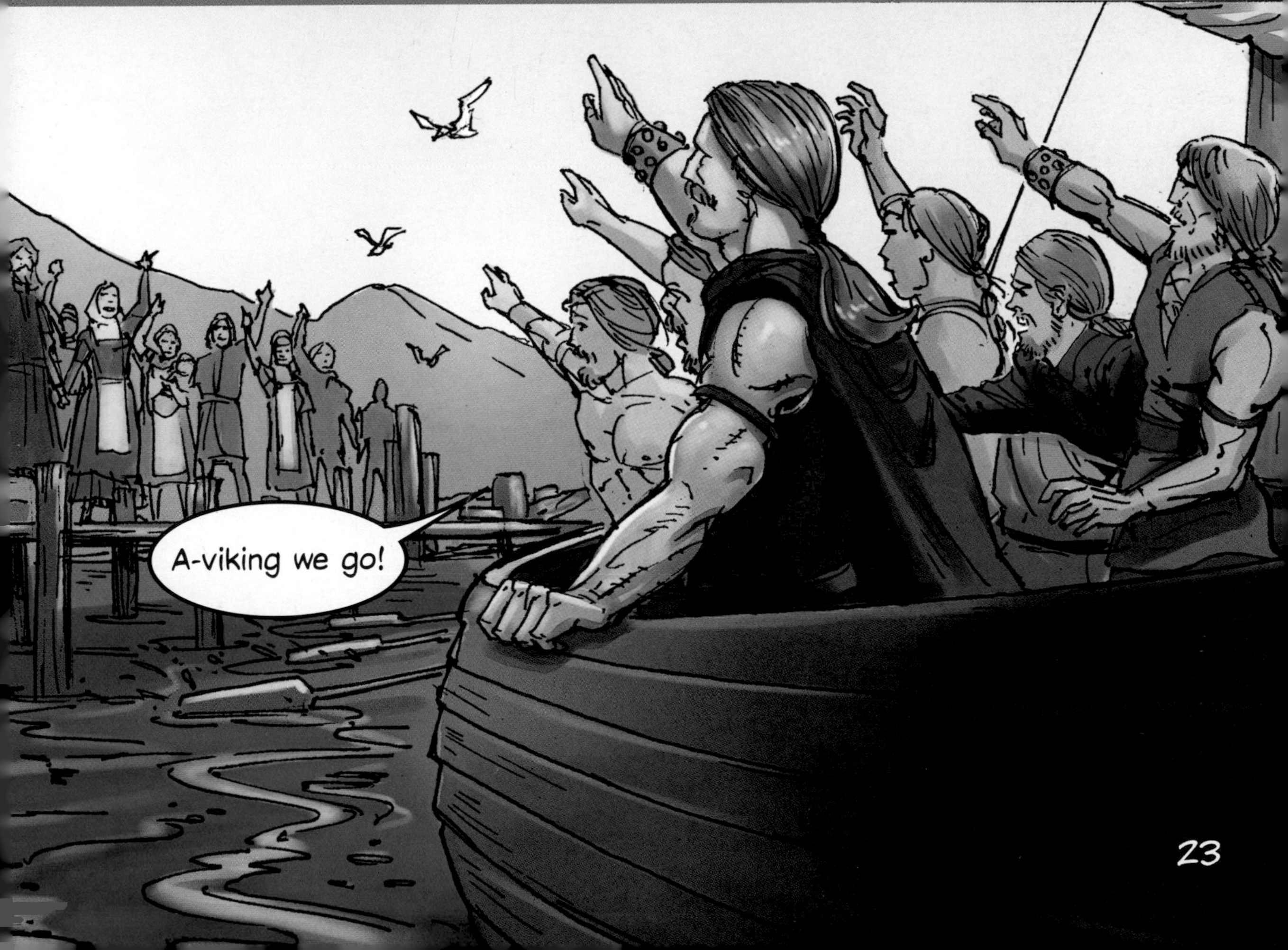
A-viking we go!

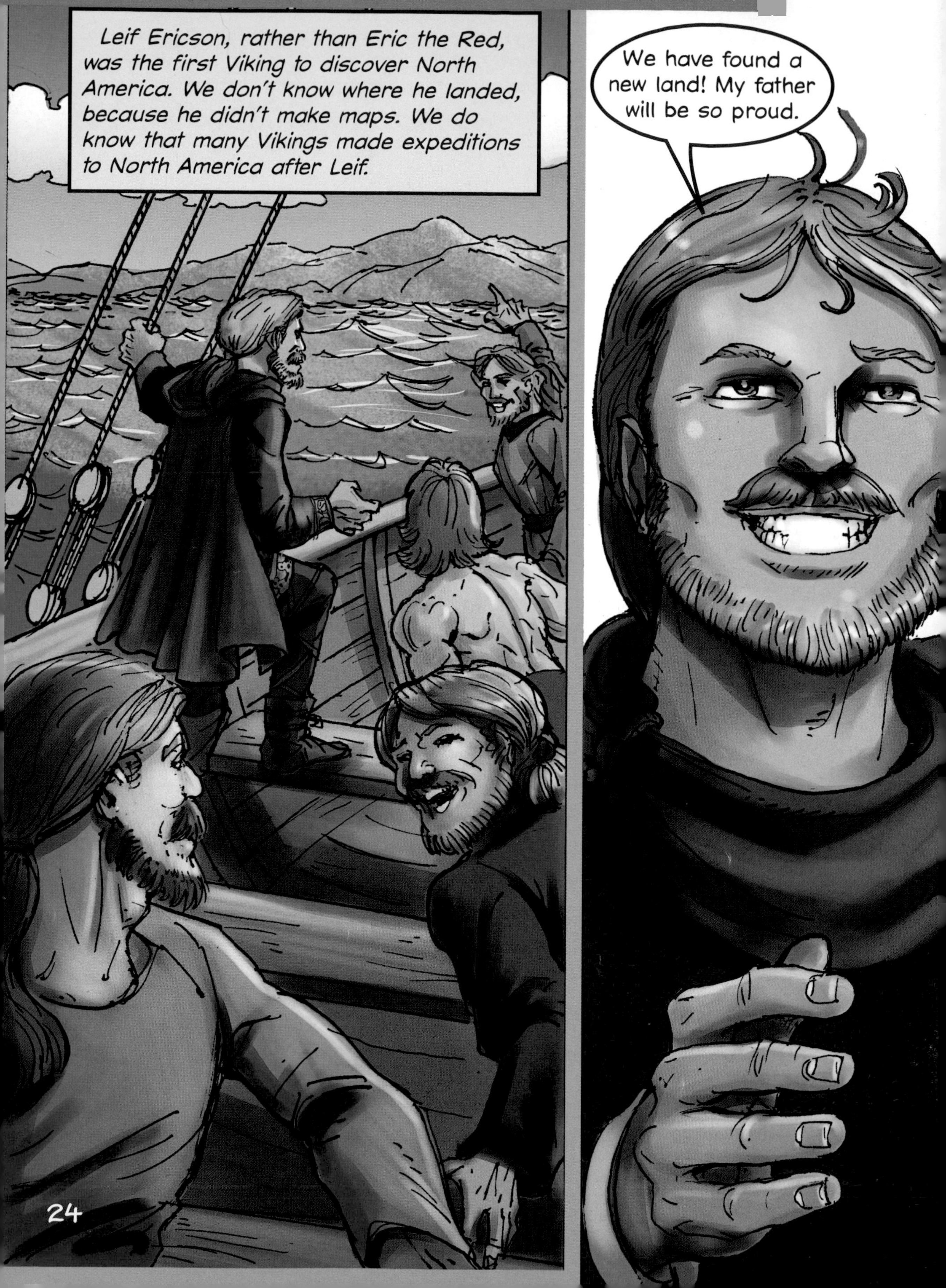
Leif Ericson, rather than Eric the Red, was the first Viking to discover North America. We don't know where he landed, because he didn't make maps. We do know that many Vikings made expeditions to North America after Leif.
We have found a new land! My father will be so proud.

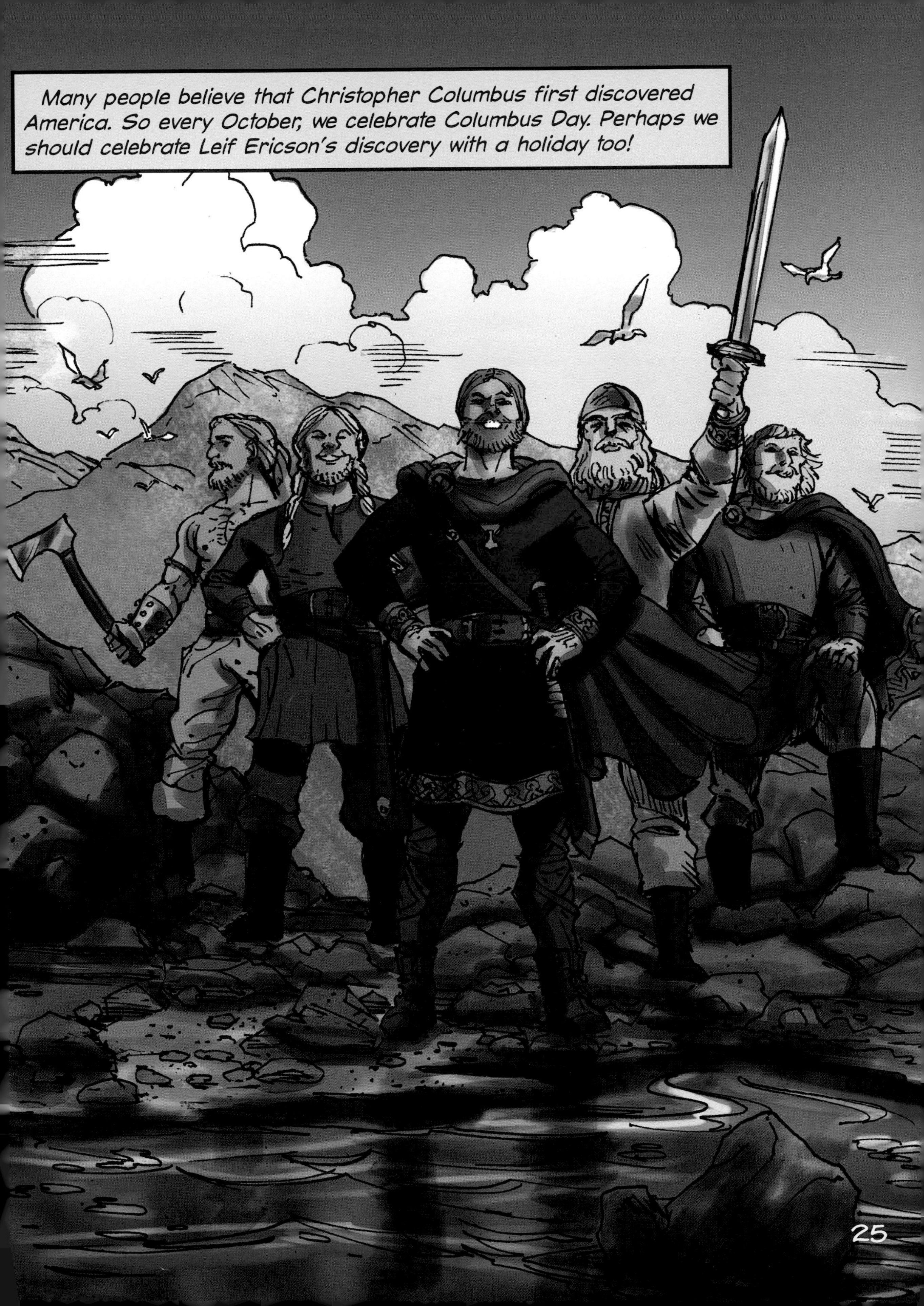
Many people believe that Christopher Columbus first discovered America. So every October, we celebrate Columbus Day. Perhaps we should celebrate Leif Ericson's discovery with a holiday too!

The Vikings were so important in the history of Europe that the time period from A.D. 750 through A.D. 1050 was called The Viking Age. They explored and conquered many areas in Europe and even made some of the first voyages to America.

Timeline

- A.D. 985 - Eric the Red established colonies on Greenland.

- A.D. 985-986 - Bjarni Hejolfsson, an explorer from Iceland, saw the Americas.

- A.D. 1000-1001 - Leif Ericson followed Bjarni's route to the Americas and discovered the new land he called Vinland.

Edgar the Pacific being rowed down the River Dee by Eight Tributary Princes.

This engraving shows a small Viking longboat. Longboats were symbols of wealth and power.

The lands where the Vikings came from were not very good for farming. There was too much sand in the country we now call Denmark, too many forests in the country we now call Sweden, and too many mountains in the country we now call Norway. Most people depended on farming as a way to support themselves. They survived by growing their own crops and raising their own animals to eat. But Vikings were

This statue of Leif Ericson is located in Rejkavik, Iceland.

also adventurous and skilled shipbuilders. The need for more farmland, combined with the adventurous spirit and good ship building skills, made exploring and conquering new lands appealing to the Vikings.

The Vikings left their native region, which was the part of Europe that we now call Scandinavia. They traveled to Europe, Asia, and the Western Hemisphere, including parts of North America. The Vikings traveled by sea as well as by land. They were great warriors who easily defeated the people living in the lands they invaded.

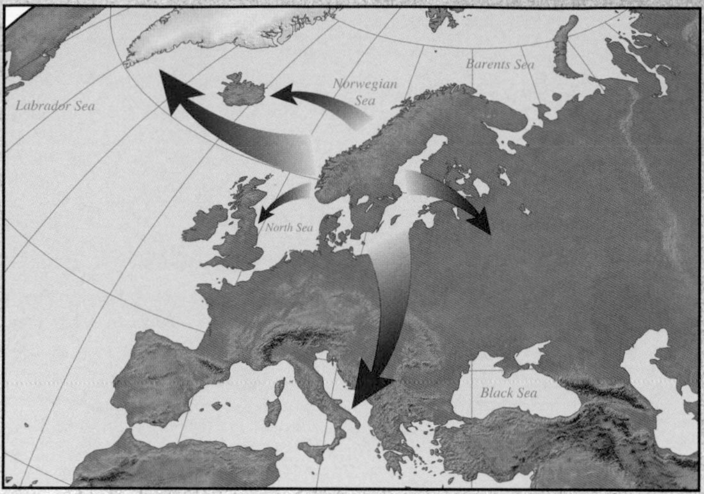

Labrador Sea
Norwegian Sea
Barents Sea
North Sea
Black Sea

These red arrows show the direction the Vikings took as they migrated through Europe.

The influence of Viking culture remains strongest in Scandinavia. Iceland remains heavily influenced by Viking culture as well. The Viking culture itself was influenced by other cultures that they encountered while conquering new lands.

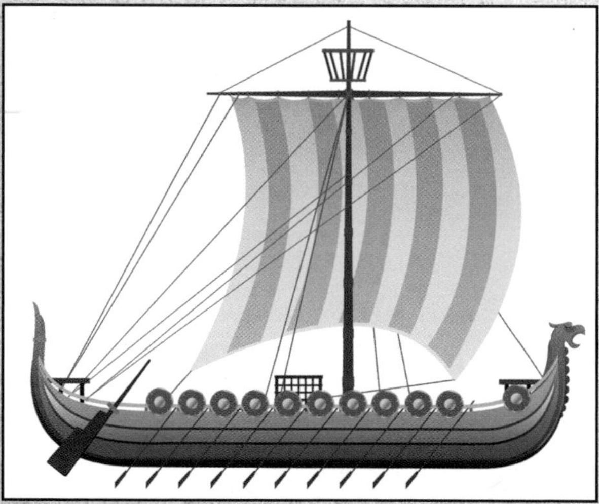

Wealthy Vikings and Viking warriors were buried in their longboats.

By the end of the Viking era, one of the biggest changes in beliefs occurred. Most Vikings had become Christians who no longer worshiped the many Viking gods. They followed the beliefs of the Christian religion. This change in religious beliefs made the Vikings more like their European neighbors.

Celctic crosses were a pre-Christian Norse cross. The Celtic cross shown here dates back to the 3rd century.

Websites

www.pbs.org/wgbh/nova/vikings

www.mnh.si.edu/vikings/

www.bbc.co.uk/schools/vikings/index.shtml

library.thinkquest.org/10949/fief/medknight.html

www.kyrene.k12.as.us/schools/brisas/sunda/ma/1Jake.htm

www.mnsu.edu/emuseum/history/middleages/knighthood.html

history.howstuffworkds.com/middle-ages/knight2.htm

Glossary

Celtic cross (KEL-tik KRAWSS): This is a cross with a circle in it. It was popular as a symbol before the Christian cross.

Eric the Red (EHR-ihk THUH RED): He was a famous Viking explorer and commander.

Frey (FRAY): To the Vikings, this was the god of the harvest and wealth.

Freya (FRAY-uh): To the Vikings, she was the goddess of beauty and love. They believed that she was the sister of Frey, and that she became the wife of Odin.

Leif Ericson (LEEF EHR-ihk-suhn): He was the son of Eric the Red and was a great explorer. He probably came to North America long before Christopher Columbus arrived.

longboat (LONG-bote): This was a long, narrow boat built by Vikings. It had oars and a sail. It was sometimes called a longship.

North America (NORTH uh-MER-i-kuh): This is one of two continents in the Western Hemisphere. It includes the United States, Canada, Mexico, and Central America.

Odin (OH-dihn): To the Vikings, he was the most powerful Viking god, who could disguise himself as a human.

Scandinavia (SKAN-duh-NAY-vee-uh): This is the area of northern Europe that includes Norway, Denmark, and Sweden. Sometimes Iceland and Finland are also included.

Thor (THOR): To the Vikings, he was the god of thunder and was the son of Odin.

Viking Age (VYE-king AJE): This is the time period between A.D. 750 through A.D. 1050 when Vikings were most important in European history.

Index

About the Author

Don McLeese is a journalism professor at the University of Iowa. He has written many articles for newspapers and magazines, and many books for young students as well.

About the Artist

Chris Marrinan is an artist who has created images for many things, including everything from billboards to video game covers! He got his start in the comic book business drawing for the comic book

publishers DC Comics, Marvel, Dark Horse, and Image. Chris has drawn many comic icons, such as Wonder Woman, Spider-Man, and Wolverine. He lives in Northern California with his two children.